Wisdom and Common Sense
for Young Adults

Kelly Ware Cross

First published by Dog Ear Publishing
4010 W. 86th Street, Ste H
Indianapolis, IN 46268
www.dogearpublishing.net

ISBN: 978-160844-595-0

This book is printed on acid-free paper.

Printed in the United States of America

FOREWORD

by Dr. Joe E. White-
Former President of
Carl Albert State College

Sometimes in the tenure of a college president you realize that a particular student has an outstanding ability and a tremendous desire to make a difference in their life and others around them. Kelly Ware Cross caught my immediate attention as one of those people with a driving desire to make the world around her a better place. She grew up financially challenged. As a result, she wants to help others avoid the same struggles she had to endure.

It was my pleasure to be introduced to Kelly. She is from a small town in Oklahoma and was taught strong core values and work ethic. I was impressed by Kelly's commitment to move beyond her current circumstances, obtain a quality education and be a positive influence for others.

During her academic years, she continuously pushed herself and her fellow students to strive for excellence in the pursuit of their dreams; and work for the opportunity to be a leader in the 21st century. I am proud to say a few simple words that Kelly has written in this book contain secrets to moving beyond mere environmental circumstances and how she has achieved this. I hope you will read this book and pattern your life whether rich or poor after Kelly's dramatic desire to give back rather than take from society. Here is one lady who has made a huge difference. Please read America.

Dedication

I would like to dedicate this book to my family and friends who have encouraged and supported my BIG dreams. I am forever grateful to the educators and mentors that have encouraged me to study and obtain a college degree. Also, several teachers at Carl Albert State College mentored and taught me so much about myself and life. In addition, I am indebted to the pastors of the BSU and Chi Alpha (both at CASC) for leading me down the right path. They were my spiritual leaders when I had none. The mission trips and outreaches we organized will be cherished memories forever. Most importantly, the Lord for always giving me a second chance and for revealing things to me slowly at the pace I could handle. I will continue to be a work in progress but I have grown tremendously over the years. It is amazing what the Lord allows us to experience so we can use those experiences to witness and encourage others.

> *James 1:2-5, "My brethren, count it all joy when you fall into various trials, knowing that the testing of your faith produces patience. But let patience have its perfect work, that you may be perfect and complete, lacking nothing. If any of you lacks wisdom, let him ask of God, who gives to all liberally and without reproach, and it will be given to him."*

A special thanks to my dear friend, Jacob Richardson for designing the book cover.

Introduction

One of the most baffling things I have discovered is that most people do not know how to manage personal finances. This can be quite frustrating; especially with the way the economy has changed in the last five to ten years. It seems like basic common sense, but amazingly enough the average American avoids common logic and reason when making major financial decisions; in my opinion, most tend to rely on their emotions when making decisions. (We all do it!) These major decisions can include buying a car, financing a home, having children, and numerous other decisions that change the financial picture of any family for years to come. A few years ago, when I was about to finish college, I had an epiphany, what am I going to do with my finances when I graduate and hopefully get a job, career and family? I decided I wanted to make valid and correct decisions that would set me up for a successful life, financially, emotionally and spiritually. I had started looking into financial services and other aspects of the financial realm. I wished that I had taken the time to study earlier on, but did not know I had interest in it. The following are a few things I have learned in the last ten years that have helped me and my family to make more thought out wise decisions regarding our expenditures each month and year. I hope that they are found to be helpful and encouraging to you. No one is perfect and we all make mistakes, but what one does once they make them is what really matters. For example, making the same mistake over and over is absurd. That is where the emotion verses logic comes into practice. Practice makes perfect. Keep trying and eventually near perfection will start showing in the horizon.

This book will contain three subchapter sections: financial insights, business insights and personal insights. I hope you find them encouraging and eye opening.

Financial insights and Common Sense

CHAPTER 1

The importance of making wise financial decisions

First things first, what is credit? Credit is basically debt or deferred payment for something. How credit is given is based on credit worthiness and a person's financial reputation, whether you have one or not. Credit worthiness is how lenders decide what you can and cannot afford based on your financial reputation and ability to pay things back. For example, say you have five hundred dollars in your pocket and what you want to buy is six hundred dollars. You know that you do not have enough to buy it. However, if it is a credit card that you are applying for with a six hundred dollar limit based on your debt to income ratio the lender knows what limit you can and cannot afford. It can be a tricky thing, banks and lenders regulating our credit. It seems with the credit crunch and millions of households living outside their budget, America is starting to take notice of debt, credit and trustworthiness of all parties involved. Being frugal is becoming the new hip and cool trend. It is an interesting relationship, the lender and the borrower. I would prefer to be the lender than the borrower. A tidbit of wisdom from scripture that has helped me in understanding this lender and borrower relationship is as follows:

Proverbs 22:7 "The rich rules over the poor, And the borrower is servant to the lender." This scripture puts the relationship in perspective for me, as a negative relationship. Who wants to be a servant to anyone else unless by choice, like a servant leader? (To me, a servant leader is someone who will sacrificially do things for the benefit of their peer group, family or coworkers instead of just making decisions based on how it affects them individually). However, in our society we want instant gratification and crave material things immediately. This is where the dilemma begins.

Many people are blessed with good reasoning skills in making financial decisions. These people might look at the pros and the cons in every situation to help them to determine the best decision, hopefully leading to the most positive outcome. For instance, in college I chose to purchase braces to fix my crooked and gapped smile instead of buying a personal vehicle. A personal vehicle was not a priority to me because I lived and worked on campus, so it would not be a necessity, but a luxury. Hence, I did not want to purchase a car. Not to mention the cost of car insurance, gas, monthly maintenance and the likelihood that it would break down; Remember, I was just a poor college kid and the only thing I could afford would likely be unreliable. Funny story though, when weighing my options I test drove a car from a local dealership and it BROKE down on me, not kidding. Praise the Lord it did then and not when I was driving off the lot with the title in my name. I was not mad; I thought it was comical the way things worked out in my favor. Back to reasoning skills, reasoning and logic will only get one so far in life. Then the rest is left up to faith and old fashioned hard work. A strong work ethic is an important quality to obtain early on in life. Hard work is one of the strongest factors in determining one's success in business and life in general.

Another basic component of setting oneself up for financial success is setting a monthly budget. My recommendation: for two to three months keep a list of EVERY penny you spend, whether you pay cash or use a credit card. This exercise can be very eye opening. Many people think that they know where their hard earned money goes, when in reality they do not. This will help a household determine how much is spent in what areas, such as: utilities, mortgage, food, clothing, vehicle upkeep, child care, and every other category. This will also help one determine what items they are purchasing that can be decreased or completely eliminated. A great example, each day if you go to lunch with a group of friends from work it costs on average about five to seven dollars a day, depending on where you go or where you live geographically. Consider this, what if you decide to take your lunch two or three times a week, big sacrifice. Annually this cut back can save about seven hundred and fifty dollars plus or minus depending on the frequency of cutting back. Obviously, not all will be transferred into your cash flow, some will go into purchasing food to brown bag your lunch at work. NICE, can you see the dollars coming back into your monthly budget to be spent on other more important things? Or a smaller sacrifice, don't buy costly beverages at each dining experience, drink water instead. This small cut back will save about eight to ten dollars a week, annualized at about five hundred to five hundred twenty dollars. (Quite eye opening indeed!) Once the exercise is over, a household can really dig deep and determine what expenditures are necessary and what can be eliminated to decrease costs.

One big thing that I learned doing this exercise, I was forgetting the money spent on emergency items. For example, say your transmission goes out or your washing machine quits working. So for good measure, be sure and leave about one hundred to one hundred and fifty dollars each month for minor emergencies. If no emergencies occur great, but if so, you are covered. This exercise is not meant to be a negative experience but a positive one. Why? Because it educates one about their household's monthly expenses, needs and wants. It can also help a household reallocate money for other things. Think, what are a few things that you or your household need or want that currently are not in the budget. This is very positive. It allows more positive, long term decisions to be made more wisely. What if you need a newer model vehicle, money for college, a restful vacation or new furniture? It can put things in the right perspective. I have learned from my experience, if I save for something and pay cash for it, I get more fulfillment out of it. Not to mention, I am excited that I do not owe anyone or pay any finance charges, because I paid for it up front with no strings attached. I do not owe a lender for it. I own it outright; it is legally mine and not a lenders. This goes back to the wisdom of understanding the lender and the borrower relationship. It amazes me how people judge a book by its cover and not by the actual situation.

When wiser more thought-out decisions are being made, more money will be available possibly for the wants in life. Personally, I enjoy traveling and fine dining with money I reallocate. Some households spend extra money on monthly splurges, every cable channel possible, weekend trips, expensive accessories, and other things that some consider regular normal expenditures, when in fact some consider them unnecessary luxuries. It is important to note, each household is different, and it all reverts back to looking carefully at the household finances and budget. What one household cannot afford another can, depending on household income level?

A few tips in making important financial decisions:

> Make sure that your significant other is onboard and an agreement is made before big purchases are made. Don't spend money that is or isn't in the budget, if you have not agreed with your partner on it. A conversation needs to

take place about when to include the other in on expenditures. For example, anything over fifty dollars or one hundred dollars needs to be discussed before purchasing.

A good rule of thumb: if you or your household are about to spend a substantial chunk of money on something, wait a week or two. You might be surprised that in a week or two, you may not even want to purchase it anymore. What a great way to avoid purchasing things that will lose their luster and appeal once the new wears off. Trust me on this.

Pray about big purchases; Make sure you have peace of mind about a decision before you officially make it. This will save lots of heartache and disappointment in the long term.

Most importantly, make decisions out of your heart not from emotions and keep God involved in decisions.

The following scriptures have helped my household and family make better decisions regarding finances, business related tasks, or personal choices.

1 Timothy 6:10-11 "For the love of money is the root of all kinds of evil, for which some have strayed from the faith in their greediness, and pierced themselves through with many sorrows. But you, o man of God, flee these things and pursue righteousness, godliness, faith, love, patience, gentleness."

Make decisions for the right reasons, not based on emotions or short term gratification, but for a positive outcome in the long-term picture. Think about the consequences of your actions, before you act or react.

Best Practice- If you are unsure of what to do, research and educate yourself about areas you are deficient in; it is not shameful but admirable because we all have short comings and fail. The important thing is to learn from mistakes. Keep your head up and continue trying to better yourself. By doing so, you will avoid mistakes that countless others make and may continue to make year after year. It can become a vicious cycle of repeating poor decision making.

CHAPTER 2

Good debt versus bad debt

It is common knowledge that there is good debt and bad debt. Unfortunately, with debt negative signs can come along and attack us. They can include: anxiousness, stress, fear, financial burden, and many others. The thing to remember is that no matter if good debt or bad debt, things have to be kept in perspective. To avoid common pitfalls, understand student loans are good debt. If one gets student loans to buy things they do not need or take trips they cannot afford than that is good debt used unwisely. There is a huge difference.

Good debt includes the mortgage for a home. Purchasing a home for your family is the first step in acquiring assets and increasing net worth. However, an example of bad use of this good debt is getting a one hundred percent loan for a home. Referring to heeding advice from our older generations, they used to save money for months or even years until they could save a big enough down payment to lower their financial burden and in-turn lower their monthly mortgage payment. Why do most people not do this anymore? It makes no logical sense to purchase a home with no down payment equaling no equity. Then if life happens or the economy enters into a downward spiral, families become unable to pay their monthly bills or even sell their home for what principle is left on the loan. It is quite sad that many lending companies do not care enough to tell their customers' about this negative consequence. Who always reads the fine print? Read every document you sign, especially those that are legally binding.

I don't blame consumers that fall into this trap. They just have not been taught or educated themselves about the entire picture around purchasing a home, what their actual payment will be, and being prepared when it comes to the worst case scenario. A home should be a secure safe place, not one that brings stress because of the steep mortgage payment. Why not buy a home thousands of dollars under your budget so you can sleep easy at night and enjoy life to the fullest. Because don't forget, with the purchase of a home comes regular maintenance, furniture and other furnishings that have to be bought. Many people purchase homes at the TOP of their budget, which in turn can bite them in the behind later. This is very disheartening because I know from experience couples or individuals go to their lender and get pre-qualified for enormous loans, which in actuality are not within their income range. Consider this, what if you lose your job, you suffer unavoidable medical issues, or go through an ugly divorce. It is chaos three hundred and sixty degrees with no end in sight. I am not a negative person, but things have to be thought out before major decisions are legally binding, as in a contract. The right decision has to be made for all parties of interest, weighing what ifs and such. Be cautious and faithful to make sound and wise decisions, circumspectly.

Scripture for thought and reflection:

Ephesians 5:15-16 "See then that you walk circumspectly, not as fools but as wise, redeeming the time, because the days are evil."

This is great advice about looking at possible outcomes and consequences before making important decisions. It is a good thing to remember that anything anyone needs help with is in the Bible. Remember, it is termed the 'instruction manual' after all.

1 Corinthians 3:19 "For the wisdom of this world is foolishness with God. For it is written, "He catches the wise in their own craftiness."

A common pitfall many fall prey to is, not living within their means. It is easy to determine if you live within your means. Research your monthly checking and savings account. Look at how much was deposited and how much was withdrawn. If the with-drawls subtracted from the deposits are a negative number you are currently over spending your monthly income. It is not rocket science, but basic math. That is when the budget and the two or three months of tracking spending come in handy to determine what and where to cut costs.

Credit card debt is a huge epidemic in America today. This is part of the reason for the credit crunch. Lenders have given so much credit to households that families across America are struggling to make minimum payments. This can be because of job loss, trying to keep up with the 'Jones', medical bills, filling a void in their life, or whatever. Don't fall into this trap. It can and will suck the life out of your household, possibly your marriage and your health. Please, if you are in debt, prioritize expenditures and cut up the credit cards to get a hold of the situation. (The average credit card debt of Americans is thousands of dollars a person, which includes averaging in those who have none and those who have thousands).

Many people buy things to fill either emotional gap in their lives, build up their self-esteem, to portray an image that everything is okay, when in reality it is not. I know this from experience. I know people that are materialist and are emotional shoppers;

when they feel bad they shop, when they are angry they shop. It is quite sad. It should not be this way. Their needs should be met without this madness. We will discuss this in more detail later.

I know for the short time that I was a financial planner, I learned about this crazy truth, people living beyond their financial means. It was frustrating for me because I was trying to help people research and study their income and expenditures with the goal of making wise decisions. This in- turn would eventually lead to financial freedom and retirement. Unfortunately, I learned many people are stubborn and do not want to make the sacrifices to have a positive life, that includes a decent retirement. (At least, the majority I worked alongside). One common misconception is that in order to be debt free and be able to save, one has to make lots of money. This is not true. It is what you do with what you have, not necessarily how much money one makes. Yes, it is great to work on increasing your income over the years of your working life, but not always an option for a small percentage of the population.

A personal example, when I was attending Carl Albert State College I worked for minimum wage twenty to twenty fives hours a week. I spent one hundred twenty fives dollars a month for braces, about one hundred dollars a month for dorm living, so much for food, clothing, tithes, etc. I chose to sacrifice a few small things so I could save forty or fifty dollars a month, which was about nine hundred dollars after eighteen months. When I graduated one semester early with my Associates Degree, this money was used to move to another community so I could obtain my Bachelors degree at a prestigious four year university. This is just an example to reinforce the fact; small sacrifices over time can lead to a big payout. Another example, if you put an initial one hundred dollars in a savings account and have fifteen or twenty dollars auto drawn from a checking account each month, after five years, it grows to one thousand dollars without interest. I used this saving technique to partially pay for two of my graduate level classes. It is amazing what a few dollars a month can become over time. Such a small amount each month probably won't even be missed. Pay yourself before you pay anything. It will pay off substantial dividends in the long term.

CHAPTER 3

Luxury or necessity

Obviously, the United States of America is a wonderful, free and prosperous place to live. Why do you think that it is such a melting pot of immigrants, people of countless backgrounds, countries and varying cultures? America has amenities that are not even available, rather-less affordable in many other cultures. We know this and yet most, in my opinion take this fact for granted. In many third world developing countries birth control, medical care, clean water, vaccinations, education, and other every day things available to Americans, are just not an option (unless one is affluent or wealthy). This is a sad truth that wonderful numerous non-profit, government agencies and religious organizations are trying to change.

It comes to reinforce my next topic. What expenditures are necessary and what are luxuries (not necessary)? Now, hear me out. I understand that many things available one can afford, but where is the line drawn to what is a staple and what can potentially be cut out temporarily or for good. Basic necessities include: food, shelter, clothing, medical and education. Obviously, this is an abbreviated list, but it includes many sub-accounts under each category. This brings about the opportunity to reference the two or three months you recorded your daily expenditures. This is a great time to reevaluate items on the list that seem frivolous or out of one's budget. An example, regularly drinking premium coffee that is four times the cost of a regular cup of coffee. It is great to splurge on certain things, but when it becomes more frequent than not, it could be deemed excessive. You decide, what is more of a priority, saving money or getting your caffeine fix? Not harsh, but very eye opening. The same is true for other things such as manicures, pedicures, massages, monthly haircuts and other high ticket services or items. Once again, it is great to splurge occasionally on an anniversary, birthday, etcetera, but what is excessive? You decide.

This is the part where most people, especially women throw a tantrum. Do your shoes, belts and purses all have to coordinate for every outfit? Come on, think about it. I am like any normal woman who wants to look nice and coordinate but it can get out of hand. I know personally people that have a different belt, purse and shoe for each outfit. This is pretty ridiculous if you ask me. How about buying a basic brown purse, black purse or a couple other affordable ones that go with about everything in your wardrobe? I know that expensive purses are popular right now, but do you really need or can afford a four hundred dollar purse? It will not last forever; it is made of synthetic man-made fibers that will fall apart. It is sad some people find their worth in material things.

Men can purchase expensive fishing equipment, camping gear, a boat, recreational vehicle, gamble, the skies the limit. There are many expensive toys and hobbies that men enjoy. For women, it can be a lot of little things that can equal an expensive lifestyle. Now, I am not saying you can't have a nice life. Take things in moderation and you might be surprised that the quality of life for your family will improve. Do you need a television in every room or a computer in every room? Not necessarily. I remember as a child we did not have but maybe ten channels on our rabbit-eared antenna television. We lived in the country. We could not get cable and could not afford it anyways. We played outside, climbed trees, played house, and used our imagination. Free and priceless creative energy was used instead of driving up the electric bill.

I say this to reiterate the point that life does not have to be filled with endless possessions or with costly things for yourself or your children. How about going to the park, taking a walk or whatever? It is actually becoming acceptable to be cost conscious these days since the economy is in such turmoil.

Eating out can be very expensive especially for a family of four or five. Choose wisely if you do go out. Many restaurants have family nights, when children can eat at a reduced price or for free. Now remember, the restaurant is probably banking on the fact that because the kids meal is free that you will spend more on your meal. You don't have to though.

There are discounts and coupons on the internet, phone book or retail outlets. You might be surprised what is offered. I am not ashamed to say I use coupons on occasion. There are several online sights that offer free printable coupons. The main thing to remember is to not print coupons on items that you do not already purchase, and then it is not really a savings but a lure to try something different. Also, there are many coupon books you can purchase at local retailers for your city and surrounding areas; they usually include buy one get one free items, discounts on travel, photo finishing, hair cuts, and even movie tickets.

Learn during these times how you can make little changes that can lead to big changes in the long-term. I wish you the best. Remember these scriptures along the journey:

Joshua 1:9 "Have I not commanded you? Be strong and of good courage; do not be afraid, nor be dismayed, for the Lord your God is with you wherever you go."

John 16:33 "These things I have spoken to you, that in Me you may have peace. In the world you will have tribulation; but be of good cheer, I have overcome the world." Jesus is speaking to his disciples. The book of John is a great book to read about knowing God, believing and bearing witness.

I write this to get a point across, God knows every hair on our head. He cares for you and your daily life. God is not supposed to be some distant being that does not care about us. He is ever present and constant. He is everywhere at all times. He cares about your financial future, your daily life and your personal well being. He cares and is present, even when we think no one else cares or is there for us. That should be encouragement enough to keep your head up through the tough times and the good.

Business insights and commonsense

CHAPTER 4

Do what is right

A basic principle in business is doing what is right. Sounds easy, right? Not necessarily. This will definitely set you apart from your colleagues and business partners. An unfortunate fact is most people are only looking out for themselves. Some may see this as admirable, not me. The best thing to do is to do what is right for all parties involved. The best advice I can give from my limited years in the working world, are as follows:

> Make business decisions based on the facts at hand, not emotions and who is involved. You should not go wrong when making decisions based on the facts of the situation. The main thing is that all the cards are on the table to make an informed and wise decision.

If something feels wrong in your gut about the decision or partnership at hand, listen to your instinct. Chances are, you are right and by listening to your inward voice you can avoid trouble and turmoil in the future.

Don't make decisions because everyone else says it is the right thing to do. Don't judge a book by its cover. The cover may just be tattered around the edges but inside is gold. Take a look at the entire situation and remove yourself from the minute. What does it look like from a three hundred sixty degree angle? The fact that you are contemplating what is right or wrong is a step in the right direction.

Strive to make decisions that will equal long-term success not just success for the short-term. I have worked with people that make split second decisions because it helps them short-term and it ended up backfiring weeks or even months down the road.

Competition can be a good thing, as long as everyone is playing fair. Unfortunately, everyone probably will not. We are all born with a selfish sinful nature. We are taught to look out for ourselves and not anyone else. However, competition can create an exciting atmosphere of accomplishment and team spirit. I am a very competitive person, as long as the competition serves my work group.

Care first, and then ask for business. Build rapport through time and regular interactions. I have learned that the best way to make lasting relationships with customers, friends, co-workers or anyone for that matter, is to genuinely care. Sounds very corny, but hear me out. Also, people value their name, if you can learn and remember names, it will serve you well in life. People are surprised if you remember their name next time you see them. They might think who is that? How do they remember me? Some great responses come from the little important things.

Find a common denominator with people you have a relationship with, business or personal. Everyone has something in common with everyone else. Talk about things that matter to that person. You might be surprised by the conversations and insights that you are given. You may even start to have a passion for the things they do. I know I have learned something from almost everyone I have a relationship with and it is inspiring and exciting.

One of the most important things you can do is reward and recognize your employees. Also, show your friends, relatives, and others who are important to you, that you value and appreciate them. A pat on the back and an acknowledgement of a job well done goes a long way. It can also encourage them to continue with their successful habits to see what else you will do to show your appreciation and respect.

Lastly, but most importantly conduct your business with character, dignity and respect.

Psalm 37:37-38 states, "Mark the blameless man, and observe the upright; For the future of that man is peace. But the transgressors shall be destroyed together; The future of the wicked shall be cut off."Basically, those who are good and honest will have a wonderful future with peace.

CHAPTER 5

Do more than is expected

A basic component of being successful in business and life is a strong work ethic. When given a task at work, do more than is expected. Whether you work for someone or own your own business, do everything with excellence and confidence. It does seem to come easier for people who own their own business, because it is their personal company. Its success lies solely on them and their employees' performance. I respect small business owners for having courage to follow their passions and interests and start a risky endeavor of opening a business.

Another component of being successful includes going above and beyond your job title. This can lead to other opportunities, such as job promotions, pay increases, and in turn, a better life for you and your family. Also, a passion for your career choice usually leads to a job well done at a lesser personal cost. Everyone should enjoy the job they are doing, if not, they may need to consider finding a job where they can excel and prosper. I am almost certain; most do not want to work with people who do not pull their own weight and contribute to the goals and visions of the company or group. This is basic business mechanics. That is why there are opportunities for coaching members of the team towards performance and completing a job accurately.

Another component of doing your most excellent work includes, not making decisions that go against your core values. When I graduated college, I had several job opportunities that seemed great on the exterior but when researching the company and the company's core values and mission statement they did not align. Needless to say, I have declined numerous job opportunities because of that reason. Who wants to work for a company that does numerous things you do not agree with morally or for whatever reason? Now that is an extreme example, but you get the point.

Core values are the values that are formed before say age eleven or twelve. That is why it is so important to instill values and positive influences in your children when they are growing up. Don't wait until they are teenagers; it is much harder then and more painful because they have already set their core values and watched you for guidance and moral stability.

Many learning opportunities arise when stretching your skills and job tasks at work. An important thing to keep in mind, don't over stretch yourself. One person can only do so much. Set boundaries if you have to, don't become a workaholic. Your family will not remember the long hours you work, but how many of their important moments you missed. Think about it. The world is a wonderful place full of things to learn and achieve but don't let that become your driving force in life; it will possibly lead to heartache and pain.

If you need organizational skills or computer skills take a class at the library or local community college. They do offer some that are affordable and informative, some are free of charge. Anything that will give you skills that you don't currently have or just want to improve on is time and money well spent. Again, check your budget and ask your employer. Your company may provide reimbursement for some classes and activities that will give you a more diverse skill set.

A quick note: By doing more than is expected of you could eventually lead to a different role in a different company. It is after all a small world if you think about it. Networking with others and in every day life can be priceless. I am amazed at how many people have crossed my path in the last ten years. One of my gifts is remembering faces and sometimes names. It is really fulfilling to see someone I know excel and have passion for life and their job. It is amazing to see them years later living out their passion with more responsibility and a title of respect and honor. I hope people would and could say the same about me. I will continue to reach for things that I have a passion for and encourage my spirit.

CHAPTER 6

Make the touch decisions,
it is part of the entire picture

This is not to dismiss Chapter 4- do what is right. In most cases, making the tough decisions, means doing what is right. Hard decisions are part of life and include the business side. For example, with the declining economy many companies have to make tough decisions surrounding layoffs, profit margins, expenses and numerous other factors in conducting business. Several commendable companies instead of laying off people are offering pay cuts across the board instead of firing valuable employees. In researching my hometown, I learned that during the depression years of the twenties, colleges across the state did this instead of laying off professors. The times were hard enough and they rallied together to make ends meet. It is very encouraging and enlightening of the human condition. In difficult times, people work together.

We all remember the stories of September 11th, the bombing of the Federal building in Oklahoma City, travesty of hurricane Katrina and other awful events in American and world history. The positive thing people remember is that as a whole we rallied around each other, for the most part, and made tough decisions. We helped our neighbors, our friends and our country get through it and learned from the events.

In business, I think one of the hardest things is probably letting go of an unproductive member of the group. It is necessary at times, though. If the individual is not going to step up and do the job at hand, they are not being fired but basically firing themselves. They are doing a poor job with usually little passion or drive.

Another tough decision is apologizing for your mistakes. To me, it is part of the job. When the person at fault does not accept fault someone needs to take the high road and be the bigger person and apologize. It is a difficult thing to do and not enough people do it. When things go wrong, the person at fault should accept it and apologize. It is commendable and the right thing to do. We are all human and make numerous mistakes. Once again, what we do with those mistakes and how we learn from them is truly what matters.

More advice about making tough decisions and holding your people accountable:

Don't tolerate mediocrity. If you do, you or your employees will not reach for excellence, usually.

If one person is infecting or bringing the team down, respond accordingly. Coach, teach, do what is necessary to help them gain the confidence and skill base to succeed. If that does not work, make the hard decision. The person may not be working where they can utilize their skills.

A huge thing- Do not show favoritism. It seems simple but for some it is not. Side note: do not try to gain brownie points with the boss. It is at times disgraceful and annoying. Besides, your work should speak for itself. Obviously, you need to keep track of your performance for annual reviews but don't be boastful, if you can help it. This shows that you might be insecure in yourself and have to pat yourself on the back. It feels much better if it is coming from someone else. Trust me on this.

Whenever possible, be peaceable with everyone. Try to get along with everyone. Now, I know not everyone is easy to interact and work with on a regular basis. We all deal with hard headed and frustrating people. Do the best you can.

Hebrews 12:14 states, "Pursue peace with all people, and holiness, without which no one will see the Lord."

Matthew 5:9 states, "Blessed are the peacemakers, For they shall be called sons of God."

A brief summation of this chapter, make the hard decisions when necessary but keep in mind to do your most excellent work and success will be present in your life. If not presently, than I am certain it is very near in your future.

I Peter 3:10-11 states, "For He who would love life And see good days, Let him refrain his tongue from evil. And his lips from speaking deceit. Let him turn away from evil and do good; Let him seek peace and pursue it."

Personal insights

CHAPTER 7

Avoid unnecessary worrying

In today's economic turmoil, most media outlets: radio, newspaper, television and the likes are giving society many things to consider worrying about constantly. This is a complete waste of time. The economy is something in my opinion that is not within our perimeter of changing, immediately. The United States economy is global and many countless things determine what way the economy will go. I think the best thing we can do is focus on what we can do in our own lives, and not worry about things that we cannot change. It reminds me of the very popular serenity prayer.

This can be a very debilitating thing, to worry about things and even people that we have no control over. Yes, one person can make a difference, but one has to be realistic and not become radical about things that our out of our control. Please read the following scriptures to help keep perspective: Jesus is speaking..

Matthew 6:25-27 "Therefore I say to you, do not worry about your life, what you will eat or what you will drink; nor about your body, what you will put on. Is not life more than food and the body more than clothing? Look at the birds of the air, for they neither sow nor reap nor gather into barn; yet your heavenly Father feeds them. Are you not of more value than they? Which of you by worrying can add one cubit to his stature?

Matthew 6:32-34 "For after all these things the Gentiles seek. For your heavenly Father knows that you need all these things. But seek first the kingdom of God and His righteousness, and all these things shall be added to you. Therefore do not worry about tomorrow, for tomorrow will worry about its own things. Sufficient for the day is its own trouble."

These scriptures are helpful to understand that one cannot change anything by worrying about it. Worrying will not add stature to us, it is just a distraction and a negative aspect of life, if one is not careful. Avoiding worrying can help keep things in perspective and free up time to think about positive things and making sound wise decisions. DO NOT WASTE ENERGY OR TIME WORRYING.

Philippians 3:8 "Finally, brethren, whatever things are true, whatever things are noble, whatever things are just, whatever things are pure, whatever things are lovely, whatever things are of good report, if there is any virtue and if there is anything praiseworthy-meditate on these things."

Basically, think more about positive things than negative. Yes, negative things happen to everyone but if you magnify the positive the negative tends to consume our thoughts less and less.

Proverbs 16:24 "Pleasant words are like a honeycomb, sweetness to the soul and health to the bones."

Sounds like positive speaking is good for our health and our soul. Think on these things.

CHAPTER 8

Seek wise counsel

The best advice and most profound advice I was ever given on debt and how to go about gaining material things came from my grandfather, Lloyd. He told me several years ago that the best things in life are those that are paid for free and clear. Why? Because you are not bound by them and the pursuit of gaining them is not detrimental or adverse to your long term financial or physical health. You don't have a monthly payment to worry and think about constantly. My grandfather is a very wise man that I look up to immensely. I would love to pick his brain and gain more insights from his long blessed life. Not to say he has not experienced trials and hard times, wise and successful people have and do on innumerable occasions. He is a veteran who served our country while in the Marines. He continues to serve his area's local communities by volunteering his time and energy into helping others, whether widows or able bodied individuals. He has the heart of gold and character that anyone would be lucky to aspire to emulate. A word to the wise, heed advice and exhortation from our older generations. They are not just talking; they have been around the block a number of times and know what life is like and how to prevail. Hence, they are around to tell us about it.

I know when I was in high school, one of my classes visited a local nursing home. I thought that was the coolest thing we did. Listening and learning from another generation about how the world operates and what they learned along the way. Sounds like priceless information that need not be taken lightly. If you have not taken the time to do this, it is a great experience for anyone but definitely for children and young adults who are molding their core values and interests. LISTEN TO OUR OLDER GENERATION, they know what they are talking about; they have experienced similar things.

Another great tool for gaining wisdom is reading the book of Proverbs. I suggest reading one chapter each day, corresponding with the day of the month. For example, if it is January 1st read Proverbs chapter one. It is a great book of wisdom in the middle of the Bible. Coincidentally, it has thirty one chapters. Enjoy and learn from Solomon, Agur and King Lemuel. It is about character, wholeness and getting values straight. It is a very easy read, indeed.

Wisdom can come from many sources. For instance, I seek counsel and advice from friends, wise relatives, former college professors, teachers and spiritually mature church friends. People you admire and trust are great sources of confidence and admiration but also to counsel with about major decisions and life's touch choices.

The most important counsel I receive is from the Word of God and through time of prayer. I know there are many critics of this practice. Who cares? It works for millions of people around the globe. Why not try it too? The important thing is to keep religion out of it, this is about relationship. Through out my life, I have dealt with people who have been used, abused and treated poorly by people that go to church (people that acknowledge publicly they are Christians). Christian means to be Christ like, not mean, hurtful or abusive. It is a sad truth, but just because someone goes to church does not make them a follower of Christ. Please do not let hurt feelings, a bruised ego or past experiences keep you from the best life you can live, one with Christ as your Lord and Savior. The best part, a relationship with him is easy and within your reach. Don't stop reading yet. God is not through with you, no matter what age, religion, race, greed, whatever, the only Living God has a plan and purpose just for you. That should make you feel quite special, because you are.

I know for me personally, my life did not begin until I asked Jesus Christ into my heart and life, when I was eleven and half years old in a small country church. I asked him to forgive my sins. I acknowledged that he had risen from the dead after three days and I told him that I would do my best in this life he gave me, no matter what. You can do this too.

These scriptures will help you with the process; some refer to it as Romans Road to Salvation:

> *Romans 3:23 "For all have sinned and fall short of the glory of God.*

> *Romans 6:23 "For the wages of sin is death, but the gift of God is eternal life in Christ Jesus our Lord.*

> *Romans 5:8 "But God demonstrates His own love toward us, in that while we were still sinners, Christ died for us."*

> *Romans 10:13 "For whoever calls on the name of the Lord shall be saved."*

> *Romans 10:9-10 "that if you confess with your mouth the Lord Jesus and believe in your heart that God has raised him from the dead, you will be saved. For with the heart one believes unto righteousness, and with the mouth confession is made unto salvation."*

Revelation 3:20 Jesus speaking., "Behold, I stand at the door and knock. If anyone hears My voice and opens the door, I will come in to him and dine with him, and he with Me."

John 1:12 "But as many as received Him, to them he gave the right to become children of God, to those who believe in His name."

Congratulations, now you have millions of brothers and sisters in the body of Christ. Please be sure you get involved with a local church, read your Bible and pray for God to continually reveal Himself to you. Salvation is the best decision anyone can make in their entire life. Because with Christ all things are more than possible including: happiness, peace of mind, confidence in self and everything else one needs to live a prosperous and fulfilling life.

CHAPTER 9

Closing comments and advice

First and foremost, be true to yourself and your dreams. Don't give up on your dreams because life happens. Everyone has a purpose in life and a course that will lead to fulfillment and happiness. Remember though, that it is a process and missteps along the way are a given. Don't give up, keep walking. Pretend that God is leaving bread crumbs for you to follow. Some may not show as prevalent, but don't stop trying to follow the right path.

In business, do more than is expected of you and complete your job duties with excellence and continued focus.

Be cordial, respectful and genuine with everyone you have a connection with, whether business, personal, romantic or whatever. All relationships require attention and work. Great advice, if you are at odds with someone, go to that person and ask for forgiveness for anything you may or may not have done. This will bridge the gap toward a more positive and an unbroken relationship.

Also, be respectful and heed elders' advice and correction, when wise and sound. Grandparents, aunts, uncles, family and friends, who care the most about you will hopefully give you the best advice. I know for me, some of the best advice I have been given (other than the Word of God) is from mentors, professors, church leaders, and other wise individuals who have life experiences.

I want to personally thank everyone who has purchased and read this short booklet. It has been a dream of mine since I graduated with my undergraduate degree to publish something of substance. When I was younger I wanted to be a missionary but was not called to go abroad. I told the Lord I would do my best to reach those in my realm of influence. I continuously make mistakes, say and do the wrong things but God knows my heart and motive. Obviously, I am young, but wanted to share insights and perspectives that have encouraged and helped me in my journey to finding my dreams, aspirations and inner self. Much thanks and appreciation! May God bless you, your family and your efforts.

9 781608 445950